Quit Your Job in 6 Months

Book 3: Your First 10,000 Email Subscribers (How to Get Them, and How to Treat Them)

By: Buck Flogging

www.QuitN6.com

Publishing services provided by **Archangel Ink**

ISBN: 1942761503
ISBN-13: 978-1-942761-50-1

Companion eCourse

There is a companion eCourse to this book series with over 10 hours of material. Find out more by going to www.QuitN6.com.

Disclaimer

By reading this book, you are guaranteed to become the most richest motherfucker ever to live ever.

I'm kidding, I'm kidding.

By reading any of my books or enrolling in one my courses, you are obviously not guaranteed to succeed. I do everything in my power to give you the most accurate and foolproof information possible, but that should not be interpreted as a promise or guarantee. No one could ever make a promise or guarantee like that. I have had success myself, and I believe that some of the tactics, strategies, and practices that I used are applicable to many others looking to launch and operate a successful business, which is why I'm sharing that information. But I can't make any promises.

Any business, financial, or vocational decision you make is something that you do at your own risk, and you are ultimately the one responsible for the positive and negative outcomes of those decisions. You should perform your own due diligence and use your own best judgment prior to making any investment decision pertaining to your business. By virtue of reading this book series or interacting with any portion of www.QuitN6.com, you agree that you're fully responsible for the investments you make and any outcomes that may result.

Table of Contents

0.2% Optin Rate

"With this page I get a 50% optin rate," he said, as I watched his video on YouTube.

I didn't know who this dude was. I don't even remember now. I have no idea how I even ended up on his video. Despite operating an internet business—a successful one at that—I never ever watched internet marketing videos of any kind. I was "following my passion." I didn't have time to fiddle around with internet marketing. Internet marketing even seemed to be at odds with the integrity that I was trying to display in the presentation of my ideas.

But here I was, watching some young punk talk about creating something I'd never heard of before—"lead pages."

In his video I watched as he put a picture of some beach scene on a page, and then threw in a little subscribe box with about two sentences describing what was on the other side if you entered your email address. It took him only five minutes to put this page together and get it live on his website.

But it got my attention. I just couldn't believe. I couldn't believe that he got *half* of the people that viewed that page to actually enter their email addresses. I had operated a website that had received a few *million* visits, yet I only had 3,000 email subscribers!

It's true. At the time I was getting about 5,000 visits to my site per day, and I was only getting 10 email subscribers per day on average, a 0.2% optin rate. This means that it took me 500 visits to get a single email subscriber. But this kid, with a little beach scene and a box in the middle, was getting 250 email subscribers per 500 people that visited that page? You gotta be kidding me.

This was a major revelation, and a turning point in my existence as an internet entrepreneur. While visitors to my blog were very engaged, and I had built tremendous trust, it was troublesome that I couldn't get in touch with people on demand. I'd experienced the power of having a list many times, as I had an old list of about 1,000 people that had bought one of my $20 eBooks. I'd come out with a new book, email that list, and within an hour I'd sell $1,000 worth of whatever I was offering—even though many of the people on that list had subscribed years ago.

And so I went for it. I…killed…my….blog.

In its wake was a simple picture and a subscribe box. As I relentlessly tweaked and tested, I found that the more minimal the design and the fewer words of text, the higher the conversion rate. I never was able to get crazy conversion rates, but I did get over 20%, which was exactly 100 times higher than it was before. On 500 visits, I got 100 subscribers instead of just 1. And while traffic tanked, I managed to double a subscriber base that had taken me years to build in under two weeks. Within a year my number of active subscribers had gone from a little over 3,000 to just under 20,000. All without writing a single blog post! Amazing.

Perhaps best of all, I could now take new visitors completely unfamiliar with me beyond maybe hearing me on someone's podcast or reading a blog post of someone's about me, and start them off at the beginning. I created a step-by-step 24-part series (that I called a "Free eCourse") that told them everything I wanted them to know in the right sequence. It was perfect for me and my subject matter in particular, because skipping straight to conclusions without the explanation of how I had come to those conclusions sounded bizarre to new visitors. And I'm certain most of them read something that sounded too wild to fathom, causing them to quickly bounce and never return. But not with my eCourse.

I also trained them up on opening my emails and getting great stuff—pure information and entertainment without anything salesy. Sure enough, over 40% of subscribers opened all 24 emails. Epic.

And so, when I email them today, even a year after they've gone through the course, they open them up and read them carefully. My open rates aren't quite as high as they used to be, but they are still considerably higher than 30%, which, by industry standards, is still considered excellent. That's with neglect, as I've pretty much moved on from that site completely since I've grown bored of it.

I discovered something that so many people had discovered before me, but that I was completely oblivious to prior to that day of random YouTube video surfing. Email subscribers are extremely powerful. That much I knew all along. But I had no idea how easy it was to get them. I had been working extremely hard to get hardly any. All along I could have been getting even more without doing any real work for it at all.

More importantly, with effective lead capture in place back on my website, I knew that the work I did do to get people to my website would result in hundreds of email subscribers. I ran a free promotion of one of my books for five days and got nearly 1,000 that week. I participated in a large online summit, and in the 48 hours after my talk aired I got 500. I'd slap up a guest post or appear in a podcast somewhere. Boom. Another 100 subscribers. It was awesome. I got so much more out of the work I put into it. Before I was writing several blog posts every week just to keep my rate of ten per day from falling even lower!

Even today, with absolutely zero effort, I still get a minimum of 20 email subscribers every single day, seven days per week.

Of course, I used this new knowledge to launch a much smarter business, and managed to snag 75,000 email addresses in the first year, with projections to scoop up twice that many in the next 12 months.

Just think, in the two years before I discovered the power of optimizing a website for lead capture, I got fewer than 4,000 email addresses. In the two years since, I'll get close to 200,000!

Except in rare circumstances, I strongly suggest that you just focus on capturing emails, especially if you're just starting out. There are so many advantages, especially armed with the focus on RPS (Revenue per Subscriber) that you picked up in Book 2, such as:

- Being able to guide people that find you through a very smart and intimate experience, all in the perfect sequence
- Being able to communicate with your entire following on your terms, on demand
- Saving tons of time and money on website design
- Being more motivated to drive traffic to your website
- Having much more precise financial numbers with which to make important decisions regarding advertising, the value of activities you do, and so forth

The rest of this book will be dedicated to how dafuq you get email subscribers and what dafuq you do with them once you've got them for best results.

Most Desired Response (MDR)

My buddy Steve Scott was the first person I ever heard use the phrase and acronym MDR (most desired response). Luckily I was recording! You can listen to our conversation here: http://bit.ly/1WSAfix.

The concept of MDR is basically to identify what action you want your web visitor to take when they arrive on your site. It's a stupidly simple, obvious thing, but so many people fail to think that way when they go to create a website or page. That's why I had such poor optin rates and wasted so many millions—literally *millions*—of visits that I worked so hard to get. I had tried to get people to perform my most desired response—entering their email address—but I got no results because a little optin box at the top right-hand corner and at the end of every post ain't good enough!

It's important to be firm (as Mrs. Flogging says to me frequently), and give your website visitors as few options as possible. My favorite pages are the ones with two options when you arrive. Scribe or Scram! Better to lose half or even 80% of the people and give 20% or more the full experience, laid out in just the right way.

But hey, if it's so important for people to read a random blog post that you put out that week, with references to all kinds of things that you've written about before that they haven't read, and get them to read that About page where you talk about your dog and shit, then by all means optimize the site for those actions.

Some of your visitors may grumble about having to forfeit an email address to get the good stuff, but that should be the end of the grumbling. From that point forward you can exceed their expectations to such an extent that they're floored by how awesome and cool you are.

Here are some images of great pages that are beautifully laid out for the MDR—getting those scriberz. This is literally all that is shown when visitors arrive on these pages.

This was generated by a lead capture page company called Lead Pages (www.LeadPages.net) that has this down to a science. This page was reported to convert at 72%!

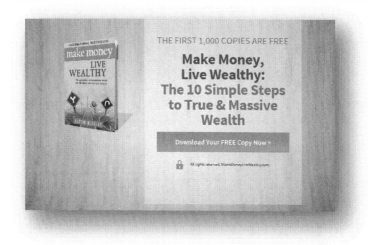

Here is the Buck Books landing page that we're currently experimenting with. Just a 30-second video with one of my mistresses and a subscribe box. Don't have any data on it yet, but this is what you do. You try things out, test, and adjust. This will get all kinds of tweaks I'm sure, such as changes to the button, the background, and whatever our split testing reveals:

Here's what internet marketing guru Derek Halpern has going on right now on his site. Looks pretty cool. I know his ass isn't putting up pages that convert at any less than 40% or so, so this must work fairly well.

Oh shit, after viewing this page I got hit with this popup. This brother's serious about this subscribing stuff, as he should be! Take a look at what I saw next:

Subscribe or die bitch! I think I'll make a popup that says that and test it out, haha.

Lastly, here's one more from one of our Buck Books events. It's amongst the highest-converting pages we've ever had, with an optin rate of over 50% for our top affiliate. Man it's nice to have all these mistresses lying around by the pool out back to take all these great pics. We made a cucumber taco together after this photo shoot:

And a little bonus for you guys. Perhaps my all-time favorite call to subscribe, while we're on this whole image-sharing kick. From www.ThugKitchen.com, authors of the best-selling cookbook of 2015 by a longshot:

SIGN THE FUCK UP

get an account, save your fav recipes & hear about the latest shit

| Email address | JOIN |

Well I hope you enjoyed the picture show.

Now go create some simple ass lead capture pages that make people do what you want them to do when they arrive.

Next we talk about what you can offer that will get them to take that action, get on your mailing list, and give you a chance to flood them with value, honesty, and fun...

Baiting the Hook

You've got a great page set up that gets your visitors laser-focused on subscribing. The looks and layout are of major importance, but it's not complete unless you give them a good reason to subscribe.

We all know the "Get this FREE eBook that'll show you how to rule the world! Get Instant Access!"

Blah, blah, blah.

While this still works to some extent, it's a tired offer no doubt, unless you find a way to spice it up a bit.

I use it gloriously (as you have probably discovered if you've visited www.QuitN6.com), but there are a few things I use to really differentiate it from others. The book looks very lifelike, and I actually hope to get pics or videos with people holding the real paperbacks when they're all released and test that. That shows that it's not one of those "books that really isn't a book" things that are like 8 pages. I also mention it's not out yet (before September 15, 2015, when the last book that I plan to write is released), which is a big difference. Registering for a hot shit book that's about to be released is different from getting something that's already been around for who knows how long. I also give away four! Not just one. Lastly, I mention it will be released on retailers everywhere. All those things put together legitimizes the book as a real book. And I get good conversion rates because of it.

My buddy Austin, as you saw in the last chapter (the first lead capture image), states on his lead capture page for his book that "The first 1000 copies are free." Pretty nifty. Evidently it worked really well, but he stopped driving traffic to that page after it was released.

So, if you plan to use the ol' "free eBook" as optin bait, you better make it look sharp and find a way to differentiate it from all the other slop out there.

What else could you use?

I love hosting big events. That's a great and totally fresh reason to subscribe. Because I offer discount books in the events I've done, and I promote discount books through Buck Books, it's a good fit. It may not be a good fit for what you do, but a subscriber is a subscriber. Even if they aren't scooped up because they love you, you might start to grow on them if your event has anything to do with what they were interested in getting a discount on.

I also offer an eCourse on one site, but it's not particularly effective. I'm sure it could be if I took the time to really sell it as a "course" with video and stuff like that, which it really isn't, so that's not happening.

I've seen free video series work very well. And that seems much easier to create than an eBook for most people. But don't do it half ass. Get a professional intro made at least on Fiverr, do it in HD if you can, and otherwise put some effort into it.

When in doubt, you can be all thug life on they asses and tell them to sign the fuck up and hear the latest shit!

You can also try giveaways, chances to win gift cards or other drawings, and other such things that we'll discuss (and that I'm testing out relentlessly in the 2nd half of 2015 with my new site www.EpicWins.us). I've even seen free audiobooks be effective optin bait. But try, if you can, to not be *too* focused on your conversion rate alone if you are really trying to build a very strong relationship with your subscribers, who you are going to sell very reputable, high-quality, expert information to on the inside. You'll devalue yourself greatly to be giving away some kind of virtual raffle ticket, and you'll fill your subscriber list with a bunch of hillbillies.

If, however, your business is designed to sell a bunch of consumer goods while they're on some kind of discount, that could be totally appropriate.

Think about it, create something very clear and simple that seems like a good match, and don't drown them with 100 reasons why they should hand over their email address. They don't need or want all that, and the more you seem to beg them for that email address the less likely they'll be to hand it over.

And when they do subscribe, that's your chance to really give them your best stuff. You want them to think, "Wow, I can't believe this is free. The stuff she's trying to sell me for $99 must be amazing!" More on that later in the book when we discuss how to treat these people once you've corralled them.

But how do you know for sure what you should offer as your optin bait, or how your lead capture page should be designed or worded? You test! You must, must, must get into the testing habit.

Testing can be tricky though. For example, you may test a lead page one day and another the following day. What's wrong with that? Each day's traffic is unique. It depends on who is driving traffic, what source they came from, and more. It matters whether the traffic is from new visitors or repeat visitors. For that reason, slapping up a page and testing it for a day or two vs. a different page isn't the perfect comparison. Too many variables. But it's a simple way to start, and it's typically better than not testing at all.

A faster and more perfect solution is what is called A/B split testing. This is cool. One visitor sees one page, and the next visitor sees the other. That way if 100 people suddenly come over from Facebook from a post of some kind, 50 will see one page, and 50 will see another. That will give you a fair comparison between the two pages, and you can compile data a lot more quickly as well.

On a high-traffic website, you can even split test things for a few hours and gather enough data to be pretty sure of which page performs better. That's great, as you can then start micro-testing very small changes such as button color, font, wording of the free offer, and more.

Whatever you do, don't test too many variables at once.

And, while testing is important, it's possible to do too much of a good thing as well. Some internet marketers go down the split testing road and get terribly lost, losing sight of what really matters, which is putting out quality content, nurturing strong connections with subscribers, and more. Do some testing, but don't lose sight of the forest for the trees as they say.

Once you feel like your offer is set and your page is designed well enough to perform up to your expectations, it's time to send them over.

Or so you'd think.

But no, that's not the right order either. Just like with the launching of an internet business in general, you want to do as much preparation as possible and get things set before you go through with the grandiose effort of driving traffic over.

So what comes first, before you focus too much on driving traffic, and potentially before you even design your site or test your lead page performance on any live traffic?

Get your email sequence all set up, thinking it through to the point of headache. While some businesses are simple with little need for complex sequences, this function is of massive significance for the right business. We'll save our discussion of that for later when we discuss how to treat your subscribers more exhaustively.

And now, the part everyone wants to hear—and what you'll desperately be ready to do if you've taken a month or two to get prepared properly—how to get people to your site. Let's dive into that beast of a topic next…

Getting Email Subscribers

Now it's time to finally talk driving traffic to your site and getting a nice, fat quantity of quality leads that will be interested in what you have to offer—from discounts to products to services to books and more.

It's not what you think. Most people think that you start blogging and asking people who find the site to like you on social media. Rinse and repeat, and, if you keep at it long enough, shazam! Full-time living from home!

Like I've mentioned before, Darren Rowse from Problogger took a survey and found that 70% of bloggers are making less than $500 per month. And approximately 85% made less than the golden point of $3,000 per month. Only around 11% actually made what we'd all consider to be a great living—$10,000 per month or more.

While blogging is a great way to generate traffic, there are two problems with it. The first is that it takes a lot of blogging before the effects kick in—not appropriate for someone starting out and wanting to achieve quick financial stability with their own business. The second is that blogging is actually a pretty difficult skill. Not everyone can be a kickass blogger. Lastly, traffic brought in by blogging usually doesn't result in very efficient lead capture. Like I said, I was getting a 0.2% conversion rate on subscribers when I was blogging, and I had a call to subscribe at the end of every single post!

In other words, except for perhaps a display ad-centric site (billboard site, to stick with my terminology), blogging is a lot of work and noise performed in vain. You'd probably be better off just writing short books and publishing them on Kindle, even if you don't charge for those books! You'll probably get them read more in the short-term, those reads would be of higher quality than a quick skim of a blog article from a first-time site visitor, and you'll even get more leads from those books than you will from visits to your blog that ride in from Google, Facebook, or wherever.

That's not to say that blogging has no purpose or value. It does. And even though I've made such a big statement against blogging with the absurd name that I came up for myself, Buck Flogging, I'm actually going to come out of blogging retirement to put some content on the QuitN6 site (just little 2-paragraph posts describing videos or podcasts mostly). I know the leads I'll gather, even if there are only ten per post, will be worth it.

But I expect to get many more from fewer hours of work from the writing of these four books. And I expect more will read them by a factor of five or more than will read the blog posts I write. I do, to be sure, have incredible promotional advantages in the book realm, and am putting money into the launch as well, but I expect to get more downloads of each book in the first 48 hours (30,000 or so) than I've gotten in 694 of my 700 blog posts, many of which have been out there for years.

And even if I was starting out from scratch, with no following whatsoever, I know that I could get to the golden point much faster by putting all of the writing I do into books rather than into blog posts. Most indie-published nonfiction books are 10,000-20,000 words these days, and I can crank out one of those every week working part-time on them. In six months, if I was laser-focused, I could crank out 26 books in 6 months, and I know I'd reach $100/day long before I got to the 26th book.

Okay, that was purely hypothetical. Please don't do that, either.

Well that'll get you thinking smart hopefully. Just because blogging, for example, can drive traffic, that doesn't mean that you should do it. Be selective in how you spend your time and attack what will deliver the fastest results per hour of your time spent until you reach a reasonable point of financial stability. Then you can add other things later that might have a more cumulative, long-term benefit.

More creatively stated, flogging before blogging.

Here are my top 10 ways to get email subscribers, and hopefully the discussion of each will give you even more ideas about smart ways to drive quality subscribers onto your list:

1. Networking
2. Affiliate program
3. Events
4. Kindle
5. Slideshare
6. YouTube
7. Social Media
8. Content Marketing
9. Giveaways (quickly moving up the list)
10. PPC Advertising

#1 – Networking

I hate to use the word "networking," as that connotes running around an expo or conference and passing out business cards like they're $1 bills at a strip club. That's a good metaphor really, as you are whoring yourself, and treating others kind of sluttily as well. I don't and probably never will have business cards. Someone asked me for one once and I said, "What do I look like, a real estate agent?" He didn't like that and actually threatened to take me outside. I had my bodyguards beat him to a pulp with Garden Weasels. We take those with us everywhere we go. Some medieval shit.

By networking I of course mean making friends and cultivating mutually beneficial relationships with people in your niche. After all, they're the ones who have put years into building up a decent-sized fanbase of people in communication with your ideal readers, clients, and or customers. There's no better way to expedite your success than to build some trust, rapport, and ultimately *friendship* with some of these people. To do that, reach out and say hi, ask good questions, be cool, and be generous without asking for anything in return. Your goal is just to be liked and to get those people knowing who you are. That's enough to derive benefits from down the road, and you probably won't even have to ask for reciprocation if you do a good job of being authentic in the first place. It'll just happen.

And don't ever fail to appreciate quality traffic over quantity traffic. When someone who's built the trust of thousands of people interested in what you're offering goes out on a limb and gives a personal recommendation to check your stuff out? That can be life-changing, and the few hundred to few thousand visitors you'll get are worth more than 10,000-50,000 visits from search engines and other common sources of traffic.

Remember, unless you have a billboard site, the goal is subscribers and revenue, not visits and pageviews. And a quality endorsement from a popular leader in your niche will outperform general traffic at least ten to one. So put yourself out there. Personal emails or @replies on Twitter are usually the best ways to connect with an individual that you know gets more attention than they can manage as it is.

#2 – Affiliate program

Along the same lines as going out there and making some pals, the creation of an affiliate program, particularly an attractive affiliate program that brings in well over $1 per click for a typical affiliate, can put you in business real quick.

An affiliate program, and one that is at least somewhat competitive in terms of what your affiliates will earn, is a great thing to have on hand when you do your networking. It's a no-brainer way for people that you're making friends with to help you out, and the best part is that your new pals will benefit from it, too. It's a win-win for everyone.

So you best be figuring out something that you can sell. Not everyone can, but it's great leverage for those who have something of value to offer. And if you have little value to offer, you can be sure that it will be tougher to succeed. As it should be.

There are many places to set up your affiliate program, or you can tie into an existing affiliate base by listing your product on something like Clickbank. Generally I'd discourage you from doing that, and creating your own affiliate tracking that you have full control over. I just started using Ontraport as a solution for sending out emails as well as managing affiliates. It's very expensive, but it's also easy to make up for that cost with the features it provides, and the relative ease of setting it up and integrating it all together. Fewer moving parts. We'll discuss it more when we talk about how to treat your email subscribers and set up proper sequences.

#3 – Events

Some of the biggest success stories I've seen online were the result of organizing and hosting an online event of some kind. I'd put this at #1 on the list, but it was such a marvelous way to build a subscriber list of 50,000+ with just a few months of work that the strategy has quickly been overdone and has lost its effectiveness.

Speaking of losing effectiveness, just a quick timeout here to let you know that many of the following things I'm about to discuss are purely tactical. And tactics gain and lose effectiveness at hyperspeed with the way things are done on the internet. So don't get too caught up or invested in any one tactic.

Back to events. An online event is basically where someone creates some kind of large bundled product, online summit with dozens of interviews, flash sale, or similar. All of the participants in the summit, or contributing authors to the book bundle or flash sale, combine their efforts to drive tons of traffic all to the same page at the same time.

People get massive value, often scooping up as many as 100 books and countless coupons, interviews, and eCourses for as little as $30. Each participant gets an affiliate link, and for each sale of whatever the bundled product may be, the participant will get 50-80% of the proceeds of the sale.

Therefore, most of the events like this pay the contributor based on the traffic they send over, not on total sales of the bundled product. That's smart, as it incentivizes each participant to work really hard to drive people over. These events are great for bloggers that don't have products in the niche the event is for, as it provides a great way for them to earn some extra income from whatever following they have.

Because these are a dime a dozen now, if you decide to give an event a shot, you better do it very professionally, not cutting any corners. An event can definitely be a great entry point for you as an online entrepreneur, getting thousands and perhaps even tens of thousands of email addresses that you can use to make a steady income thereafter—selling your own products as well as various outside affiliate offers appropriate to your audience.

As you saw with strategies #1 and #2, the idea is to have other people send traffic to your site. Events are just one particularly effective way to do it, but they are also very difficult to do right. For that reason, they sit in the #3 spot.

#4 – Kindle

As a writer that actually went to real writing school—I got a degree and everything if you can imagine such a thing—Kindle is just fucking great. I love it. Even my professors didn't know a damn thing about getting a book published, because it was so mysterious and difficult to do back in the 1990's. Now it's easier than turning in a term paper was back then. I'd have to go to Kinkos with my floppy disk, rent a computer, print it out, staple it... Oh the horror.

But now, after a little Kindle formatting and slapping a cover on that thing, you don't even have to get out of your chair to publish a book. It's pretty amazing, and I don't take this new opportunity lightly. I had literally given up on the possibility that I'd ever be a writer ten years ago. Now look at me. Living the dream.

Not only can publishing books be a lucrative portion of your overall online business, it's possible to use Kindle books as a great lead generator in and of themselves. While Kindle won't allow you to price books below 99 cents, if you publish your eBook for free on other vendors including Google Play, Amazon will typically price match that bitch to ZERO. Voila. You've got yourself a free book.

Get a little promotional help from Uncle Buck over at Buck Books, and seek out a few other promotional services out there, go nuts on social media, and have a few of your newly-acquired friends (see #1) chip in, and you should have no problem launching your book into the top #100 in the Kindle free store, getting at least a few thousand downloads during the promotion, and hopefully "sticking" pretty high in the ranks for quite some time.

Of course, you'll want at least a couple mentions of your website or a specific lead capture page where they can find out more—perhaps subscribing for an eCourse, a free video series, or to get yet another free book or something similar.

How many leads will you get from this tactic? Experience and communicating with others tells me that you'll see anywhere from 2-7% of the people that download your book make their way onto your email list.

And with a good launch into the top 100 in the free store, you could very well see over 100 free downloads per day for many months or longer. A handful of free Kindle books have gotten over 1,000 free downloads daily for over a year. So far with the *Quit Your Job in 6 Months* books, I've only seen one day below 200 downloads (currently writing this at day 34 into using this method).

For someone just starting out and needing to get some subscribers and some people reading their stuff, consider writing Kindle books, and consider publishing them as "permafree" as I described.

And, if you subscribed at www.QuitN6.com in order to get this book or others in the series, you'll know that the free book can be used to attract leads in multiple ways. Not only will I have people find this book and subscribe, I used the book to encourage people to register to get the book for free. Affiliates drove over tons of people, bringing in thousands of subscribers just like many of you.

#5 – Slideshare

Slideshare is weird as hell. I don't get it. People put together little "slide decks," and put them over on www.SlideShare.net. You can click through and see each of their slides. Whoopdie fucking doo!

Yet, for some reason that I'll never understand, Slideshare gets such an unfathomable shitload of traffic that it's currently ranked #142 of all sites in the world on Alexa as I'm writing this. 142! That's almost as high as iconic sites like Huffington Post and New York Times.

Like the female orgasm, it's one of the great mysteries of the universe.

Slideshare isn't likely to do all that much for you if you're well-established. But for new people starting out and having trouble being seen by anyone, Slideshare is a pretty sweet place to participate. The amount of new stuff published over there each day in proportion to their huge traffic numbers ensures that you'll get more views in less time on Slideshare than just about anywhere you choose to post something online.

Basically, what you do is put together about a dozen slides with a sentence on them each at most, then put a call to action at the end that links to your website or lead capture page where they can subscribe. Make sure you do something cool, cute, funny, interesting, inspiring, or otherwise emotionally-provocative. Viewing a dozen slides is unlikely to compel someone to click on your site, and is even less likely to inspire them to subscribe, so it's a tough game to play. But I bet you can get about ten subscribers per slide deck, and I bet you can put together a slide deck on someplace like Canva in a half hour with some practice.

I find it to be a great repurposing tool. Maybe you start with a blog post, consolidate that into a Slideshare and post it over there, and maybe use those slides to record your voice reading your blog post and putting it on YouTube. Every subscriber counts when you're starting out, and if you only have a few hours per day to get work done, a slide deck per day and hopefully ten new subscribers for each is probably worth your while.

Of course, the higher the RPS you have, the more worthwhile it is to do anything to drive subscribers, Slideshare included. In fact, for QuitN6, I may have a virtual assistant or "intern" or something post a Slideshare per day for a while.

Test it out for yourself and see if you think it's worth meddling with. Being stuck at zero is really tough, and I think Slideshare is a great place to at least get the wheels turning a little bit, which is why I ranked it so high.

#6 – YouTube

Close call as to which was going to claim the #5 spot. Slideshare gets a slight advantage, but only because I'm communicating with total noobs starting at ground zero. If it wasn't for that fact, YouTube would of course blow Slideshare completely out of the water. As would social media of course.

YouTube is amazing for people just starting out, primarily because videos rank so highly on Google. Google, after all, owns YouTube. Of course they want you watching YouTube videos instead of reading some jagoff's blog post about the exact same thing.

Choose good, search-engine-friendly titles for your videos and go nuts over there. YouTube is great because it is, all things considered, very easy to record, edit, and upload videos. I've gotten just under a million YouTube views in total between my several channels with extremely lackadaisical attempts to succeed over there. There was really only about a six month stretch that I was really very consistent. And I never took more than an hour from start to finish to do a video.

If you're good on camera, or at the very least you can speak okay and record screencasts or do voiceover to slideshows or whatever (or record yourself playing video games, which is all the rage these days), YouTube could be a great way to get off to a running start. Choose your video titles and tags carefully (preferably what you want to be known for, not "Kardashian titties pop out"—even though that would obviously get more views), put a link to your lead capture page in your videos and in the description, and try to post something daily or at least on a regular three-days-per-week schedule with consistency.

Just like with your writing, be yourself! And tap into people's emotions with videos that are funny, very moving/inspirational, or otherwise clever and unique if possible. And keep most of them short! Three minutes is plenty on YouTube for most things. An occasional longer video is fine of course, but generally it's better to do more videos and break them up into small chunks.

It's also important to remember that video views create a much more intimate and trustworthy connection with people that discover you. Hearing a person's voice and even seeing their face is so much more memorable. Those strong connections are what makes them great for generating email subscribers that you can count on to be engaged, interested customers of yours.

I'm also hearing that using YouTube live and pre-scheduling videos weeks before you take them live is a great way to show up high in the Google rankings. I guess live video is really Google's pride and joy right now, and you can schedule a live broadcast and have that badboy ranking near the top in Google in 15 minutes flat. I don't know much about this tactic in particular, but it could be something to take advantage of before the rest of the internet marketing world finds out about it and ruins it for everybody. Goddamn internet marketers.

#7 – Social Media

Social media is a tough one. It's great, but at the same time, it can be a real time sink. For some types of content, particularly those heavy with images and video, social media is a pretty priceless lead-generating commodity. If you want to be a food blogger or you sell clothes or something else artsy, for example, social media probably belongs at #1 on this list. Get your ass over on Pinterest, Instagram, and Facebook like your life depends on it!

But social media isn't quite as amazing for everyone, and it can take a really long time to go from starting out to really being worth your time. It's a "work hard now for rewards one, two, or even three years down the road" kinda party. Plus, I've got multiple businesses bringing in over $20,000 in revenue each month that have virtually no presence on social media. It is of little use to me, and only now are we ramping up some activity there now that we've established ourselves financially.

So don't get too enamored with social media. It isn't everything. At least not for everyone.

One thing that we are testing now that may be of particular use to a newbie starting out from absolute nothing is using an autofollow program to target your ideal customers over on Instagram. Since we started the account a month ago we've already managed to gather around 4,000 likes over there.

You simply pick someone who has a following of people that you think would also like your stuff, and then follow all of their people. Some of them will follow you back, some of them won't. The ones that don't follow you, you unfollow. Then you follow more people the following day.

This tactic was used by thousands of internet marketers to build huge followings on Twitter, myself included, but they've since banned the practice, as I'm sure will eventually happen on Instagram as well.

All in all, it's probably a waste of your time unless you have something that involves the sharing of high-quality images that can blow up over there, such as a picture of your awesome ass if you have a fitness video and personal training coaching and stuff, or you're promoting a food blog or recipe channel on YouTube or something.

We're using Instagress (the name of the software) by the way, if you want to try it out for yourself. Like I said, it's probably a dead end, and it's a little scammy, but if you're going to do it, give it all you've got or don't bother.

Oh but that's not all I have to say about social media. To me, there are really two social medias.

We've just discussed traditional usage of social media, which is to build up your own following and publicize and promote your work and ideas to that audience. To me, that's inefficient, and hence the #7 placement on this list and general dogging of it thus far. But social media is an incredible tool for networking, and as you know, networking is by far the best way to drive leads and be successful in a hurry. Don't crap on social media too hard, just use it efficiently and you'll benefit from it.

Lastly, because I KNOW you did exactly what I told you during the research phase, and you managed to identify all of the relevant groups and hangout spots on social media, such as Facebook groups, you now know yet another way to benefit from social media without having to take years to build up a following. Get in there and share your blog posts and videos if you have them, some of your work if you're a freelancer, and whatever else seems appropriate and tasteful. Just generally be cool and get to know people and see what they think about you and your stuff. It's a good way to get in front of a bigger audience than you've built yourself starting on day 1.

Also, I'm just now discovering Reddit. Of all the social media outlets, it could be the best for internet business use, it's just very tricky to maneuver without getting downvoted or banned. If you know the Reddit landscape at all, take advantage of that.

#8 – Blogging

Blogging isn't the cat's meow when it comes to lead generation, but it ain't dead by any means. I still have an appreciation for it I must say. It's a great way to improve your skills as a writer, field comments, learn what people do and don't like, get called on your bullshit, and mature as a person in general. At least, it will do that for you if you let it. It did that for me. Of course, I was really pouring my heart and soul into my blog posts, trying to write the best stuff I knew how to while sharing often quite innovative and original ideas on a number of topics. In that sense, the blogging I was doing was pretty different from your typical blahgging.

Still, the only time I really got a lot out of my blogging in terms of lead generation and sales, was when I went and blogged on someone else's site, appearing before their audience for the first time. So doing it gloriously on my own site wasn't enough in and of itself. I still had to go outside of my own little island and be heard. And when I directed people back to the site, I would have gotten a lot more out of it if I didn't have a blog there that wasn't at all optimized for lead capture.

So, starting out, I'd have to say blogging is kind of a bust unless you're publishing content on other sites outside of your own—known as "blog touring." Do some blog touring, sending people to your site, which is optimized for your MDR (most likely subscribe via email on the first visit), and you will indeed get a lot out of it.

The same could be said for podcasting, which is also a tough thing to see any results from in the short-term, but can have a cumulative long-term beneficial effect similar to blogging. Similarly, better than podcasting is going on a podcast tour, appearing on other people's podcasts, in front of their hard-earned audiences, with people eager to dart back to your site to subscribe.

Personally, if I were going to do a blog or podcast, I'd actually wait until I had an audience built first. Then I'd use that audience to help the performance of the blog and podcast by sending my people over there to check it out. I'll do this exact same thing with the QuitN6 blog and podcast. I'll draw lots of subscribers first, and then launch the podcast really high up on the new and noteworthy charts over on iTunes.

As a final note on podcasting, it is a fantastic way to do #1 on this list—network with people in your niche. Nothing beats getting on the phone with someone (well, except meeting people in person, but who the hell leaves the house?! Not me!). They'll remember you, and it's easier to get decent guests than you think, as the big fish know that appearing in front of 100 new people on a podcast is a big deal—equivalent to having a blog post skimmed by thousands.

#9 – Giveaways

Giveaways are a little trashy, but they can be used effectively and done tastefully. For example, I've seen authors who write, say, horror books, host a giveaway of a Stephen King collection. They know people that like Stephen King would really like them. So they host the giveaway, send clicks over there primarily by using method #10 (advertising), and capture qualified, targeted leads with a very high conversion rate.

I won't break down all of the scenarios and ideas that could be done with giveaways, but hopefully that example will ripen your melon—getting you thinking about finding a way to match your giveaway to the type of subscribers you want to draw.

For giveaways, it's probably best to use a program like Rafflecopter or King Sumo Giveaways to manage it for you. They've done some smart things to improve the reach your giveaway gets on social media and beyond. They actually reward people for sharing the giveaway on social media with points that result in a higher chance of winning the prize.

For a newbie just getting started, a giveaway that's well done probably belongs higher up on this list than #9. And with the resource I'm building with Epic Wins, I will have the ability to promote giveaways effectively to help you get your first several thousand email subscribers overnight.

It's a very promising prospect that could quickly jump to the top 5 on this list. But it could cost you more money than the others—money you might not have and money that, with your inexperience, may not come back to you. So for that reason it's way down on the list. Still a good thing to know about and ponder though, for future use.

#10 – Advertising

In my career, the number of advertising campaigns that I've seen a positive return on—meaning that I made more money than I spent—totals 0. None. That's also the same number of advertising campaigns that were close to breaking even. ZERO.

Advertising is a good way to lose a lot of money very quickly. Advertising isn't "dead," but, because advertising has been so thoroughly ruined by commercial entities on the internet, radio, television, and beyond—I don't have many good things to say about it. While we may be able to pinpoint who our ads are placed to with incredible precision in the modern era with advanced targeting and retargeting, and you'll discover many internet marketing gurus out there with massive boners over Facebook ads, advertising in general is so watered down you just can't expect great results with it. You might get great results, but definitely don't count on it.

Having said that, it's the dream to be able to set up a website and advertise it to success. No employees. No work. None of this other time-consuming bullshit. Just automate and masturbate.

But it's so hard to pull off that it's not worth risking time and money until you've really proven that you've got tremendous RPS.

That's right. Here it comes again. The most important component in creating a successful ad campaign is having a system in place that can turn an email subscriber into $5 or more quickly. That way you have a $5 budget to get a quality email subscriber that's comparable in quality to the one that rides in from a podcast they heard you on, a YouTube video of yours, or via the endorsement of an affiliate. Of course, advertising-generated leads are just not the same as those that have ridden over more organically via the top 8 methods in this list (giveaways excluded). And for that reason, advertising comes in at #10 on the list.

For advertising, you have more options than you realize. You can advertise on Twitter, Reddit, and all kinds of other places besides the usual suspects—Facebook, YouTube, and Google. For these forms of advertising, you will usually pay per click (PPC)—anywhere from a penny to several dollars. Of all of your options, Facebook is probably your best bet with the greatest flexibility and targeting, but some of the smaller social networks like Twitter and Reddit actually look really promising.

If I ever create a successful ad campaign anywhere, I'll let you know all about it in excruciating detail. For now, keep your wallet locked up before it projectile vomits all of your cash into advertising. I know it's an exciting thought (the equivalent of winning the lottery really, because a successful ad campaign essentially becomes a money machine where you put money in and it comes back bringing friends with it), but your money would be safer off playing slots in the beginning.

And that, ladies and gents, concludes the chapter on how to get those scriberz in. As an honorable mention I'll throw out hosting webinars. Lots of internet marketers rave about them. I always thought they seemed really weird and have absolutely zero experience with them whatsoever. So check them out if you want. If you get really good results, do tell. I hope to bring at least one webinar expert into QuitN6 to give you guys the scoop.

Now onto the even more important stuff for a noob just getting started—how to treat them, create smart sequences, and otherwise capitalize on the hard work you put in driving them into the corral.

How to Treat Them

Well obviously as soon as someone subscribes you'll want to immediately hit them up with an offer to enlarge their penis and/or breasts by 40% in four easy payments of $99.95. I mean, give the people what they want!

Come on now.

When someone subscribes, the very first thing you'll want to do is demonstrate that you aren't about selling stuff or even making money. You need to help them, be cool, provide value, and really impress them. You've already convinced them to subscribe, which is a good start, but it's not enough commitment on their part to jump right into the process of being sold something. Not at all.

Rather, you need to finesse your subscribers. This helps to sell them things later of course, but that can't be what it's about for you either. If all you really care about it selling them some shit before they move on, you won't be able to conceal that. No way. People are too smart now. They're like our mothers. They can smell peculiar odors from a mile away.

And that's good that they're smart! You shouldn't be groaning that people are no longer so moronic that they can be sold just about anything. Well, people still buy a lot of stuff, but they are probably only a tenth as vulnerable to marketing messages as they were back in the 50's when television first hit.

So what's the key? You guessed it Buckaroo. Authenticity.

Be honest, be cool, be helpful. Serve the people that find you with no strings attached. Give them a ton for free. Be willing to share the world with them. And, only because it helps you to reach out and help more people, slowly begin to escalate your relationship with your subscribers to the point of selling them something.

Then sell them more, and more, and more until both you and your subscriber have exchanged as much value from each other as possible.

If you have just one product that's crappy, you'll want to sell them that piece of crap right away when they are most excited and irrational—before they've had a chance to think critically about it and have doubts—and before the internet becomes overrun with bad reviews of your product or service.

But hopefully you realize what a poor, short-sighted tactic it is to do such a thing. Build a relationship, and sell them many somethings at many different prices. Give them everything you have to give, and they might just give you everything they have to give in return.

Just make sure to always give more than you take. Keep the ball in your court. Wow them with value every step of their journey with you all the way to the end. Help them. Change their lives. That's how you reach fulfillment, and that's how your bank account will reach fulfillment as well!

Internet marketing guru Frank Kern has a saying that I really love. He stated in a video I watched that you should try to display "shock and awe coolness" to your subscribers. He demonstrated how he did this by pointing out the radical honesty, humor, and undeniable coolness in one of his email broadcasts. He then showed the person filming the video of him playing a standing old school arcade game in his living room that he won as a bonus for that very promotion.

Shock and awe coolness.

I love that. Shock them. Surprise them. Communicate to them naturally in your, wait for it... "authentic" voice.

Another way to phrase it might be to demonstrate "radical honesty" with your subscribers. Build trust. And the only way you can do that is to earn their trust. To earn their trust you have to be trustworthy.

Geez it's so simple. But so few are doing this masterfully, because there are so few people out there that are truly genuine. And even the genuine ones have often been tainted by numbers, stats, conversion rates, tactics, ROI, and all that business stuff. It has its place, but at the end of the day it's got to be a distant afterthought to the primary authenticity that dominates the work that you do. All that business stuff you hear from me is really about just getting things set up properly, so that you can then unleash your message, skills, services, and whatever else you may offer onto the world.

Remember this. No matter how poorly you do everything else, authenticity, radical honestly, shock and awe coolness—these things can carry you a long way. One of the most authentic people I've encountered once made over $10,000 in a week promoting something to a subscriber list of only 2,000. That is more impressive than anything I've ever seen someone with a list of 100,000+ ever pull off.

The greatest "marketing geniuses" out there don't even realize they are marketing. I hope you become one of them.

And with the right email autoresponder sequences set up, you'll be able to go out there and be just that and know you're giving all your new subscribers the best experience possible—even while you're on vacation. Even while you're asleep.

Creating an Autoresponder

One big problem I had when my business revolved completely around my blogging was that my articles had to be catered primarily to the audience I had already built. A couple times per week, people that had followed me for years sometimes would check out my blog and see what the latest and greatest thoughts bouncing around in my head were.

This was a terrible problem though. To be captivating to an ongoing audience, I couldn't repeatedly explain every little thing over and over again. I'd make a quick reference to something that we had already gone over months ago, knowing that the bulk of the readers of that article would have already read that past article.

For new visitors, this was completely confusing and alienating. I made all kinds of obscure references to things that they had no knowledge of. For them, stumbling upon one of my blog posts was like walking into a movie halfway through, or starting to watch a TV series halfway through the season. There was a lot that just didn't make sense if you hadn't been keeping up with what came before it.

It was a terrible way to orient people. I needed a solution for that. I needed a way to start new people off at the beginning and walk them through a lengthy process to get them all caught up and on the same page with everyone else.

The solution? An autoresponder.

Autoresponders are really great. An autoresponder is something that goes out when a subscriber first jumps on your list. But that's just one email. You can write several emails that go out once every few days. You could write an autoresponder that contains over 100 emails if you like, taking them on whatever step-by-step journey you feel like they need to take in order to get the full experience, build up a great deal of trust and adoration for you, and ultimately become not just a customer but a loyal follower that seeks out all that you have to offer at every price point.

Here's what mine looks like. You can see I send messages out once every four days when someone subscribes, starting with a brief intro and a link to go download the free book they were promised when subscribing. Then they go on a lengthy educational process that gives them the proper introduction to one of the most important aspects of my work. I have 27 emails that go out in total:

	1	**Welcome to 180DegreeHealth!** Edit	Send a test	Delete	Copy	⚡ Send immediately	0 spam score	76.4% opened
	2	**Who am I?** Edit	Send a test	Delete	Copy	⚡ Send 1 day after the previous message	0 spam score	59.1% opened
	3	**What is Metabolism?** Edit	Send a test	Delete	Copy	⚡ Send 4 days after the previous message	0 spam score	52.5% opened
	4	**Why is Metabolism so Important?** Edit	Send a test	Delete	Copy	⚡ Send 4 days after the previous message	0 spam score	49.9% opened

Whether or not something this elaborate is appropriate for your business or not is up for you to decide. But at least you know some of the possibilities for building a strong relationship with your subscribers, so that farther down the road you can actually sell them something of greater value than the free content you're so generously sharing with them.

This is yet another example of how much work, thought, planning, and preparation needs to go into your internet business before you even launch the thing. Ideally, if you're on a "quit your job in six months" track, you'd launch your business on the 180th day and make $100 or more on the first day to achieve that, and every day thereafter. I hope I didn't imply that your business would have to be up for six months to reach that point. Unless it's poorly designed and you didn't follow the steps, build some relationships, and come up with a good launch strategy as instructed, there's no reason it can't debut to almost instant success.

Now, if that weren't elaborate and complicated enough, wait until you get a load of what's coming next. Autoresponders are great, but if you can incorporate that idea into multiple sequences based on various actions, segmenting your list and delivering an even more precise, elaborate experience, well then you're stepping into pro turf. It may sound like a headache, but hopefully I'll do a good job of explaining why it might be worth it for you to go the whole nine yards on your email correspondence.

Next Level Email Marketing—The Power of Sequences

This is some gangsta shit, and, admittedly, it's something that I am just now starting to capitalize on in my own business. As you've discovered in many of my stories of epic stupidity, I'm usually the last person to the party. Hell, I think I blogged for four years before I even started a Facebook fan page. So messed up.

So, having an autoresponder and sending out basic email broadcasts to your subscribers is great and all, but that's just where email marketing begins really. With much more advanced applications like Infusionsoft, Hubspot, and Ontraport, it's now possible to do some really advanced sequencing and list segmentation.

List segmentation is basically taking your email list and breaking it up into groups based on what they like or what they've done.

For example, you could ask subscribers whether they are male or female when they subscribe. You could then segregate the two and provide more gender-specific information and offers. Let's say you sell shoes for example. Obviously you're going to want to separate males from females. You don't want to be promoting swanky pumps to a bunch of dudes unless you can confirm that those dudes are pals with RuPaul on Facebook.

Imagine the functionality of my site www.BuckBooks.net when we're able to start segmenting our list. We'll no longer have to promote the latest bestselling romance novel to subscribers seeking books about business and entrepreneurship, and vice versa. Our competitor site, Bookbub, actually segments their mailing list into 30+ genres. You only get emailed about promotions happening with books in a genre you like. Pretty smooth. Someday. Someday.

You can also create list segments of people who have and have not opened your emails. I use this feature of email marketing exhaustively. For example, I'm currently promoting a book bundle to my Buck Books subscribers. I sent out the first mailing about it a few days prior to writing this chapter. About 10,000 subscribers opened the email, but 35,000 of them never did. So I simply resent the email to the 35,000 that didn't by creating a segment called "Book Bundle unopens" or something similar.

In the past ten hours since sending out to unopens, I've generated 1,300 more clicks on the sales page for the book bundle and more than $400 of additional sales. Noice! Not bad for three minutes of work.

The event is coming to a close in just a few days, so I'll probably send to the 30,000 people that didn't open the email that I just sent out, naming that segment "Book Bundle unopens 2," and make another few hundred dollars. And I could keep doing that to infinity.

It of course gets obnoxious after a while, and you don't want to do this too much, but for the right offer that is converting well and perfectly suited to your audience, you want to milk those unopens down to the very last drop. Using that tactic I've already been the 2nd overall affiliate for three different events in 2015, one earning me a $1,500 bonus and $9,000 in affiliate commission overall, and another bringing me $2,000 in bonus money and $10,000 overall.

It seems like kind of a scammy tactic, but it would actually be more scammy if I sent out an extra broadcast to the entire list—including those that have already read about the same damn thing. Better to potentially spook my less engaged subscribers than put too much pressure on the people that eagerly opened that first email broadcast within minutes of receiving it.

And that's really the beauty of list segmentation. It allows you to only send things out to people it is relevant for. It actually decreases the need to say the same thing over and over again to the same people, or send them things they don't care about, risking losing their interest and engagement.

But taking all that another giant leap forward, it's time to entangle your brain with sequences.

What if you had a more specific, targeted, and elaborate system than that? With sequences, you can do some awesome stuff. Stay with me here. I wish someone would have shown me this and forced me to intelligently implement it right away.

Did you know that when you send out your first email to a subscriber, about 20% won't open it and another 10-20% won't even click on the link to your free book or whatever?

Well that's annoying. What if you could just keep sending that message again and again until they finally opened up the email and clicked on the link? You can. In fact, you can keep that person imprisoned on step 1 in your sequence until they take the appropriate action. After they finally do what you know they need to do to get off to a proper start (click that link for the free book), they immediately get bumped onto a new list that has a different autoresponder sequence.

This new autoresponder sequence may give them, say, 5 emails delivered over 3 weeks with some great content of yours. Your best shock and awe coolness stuff. At the end of that, you finally reveal that you have something for sale. Prior to that they didn't even know, which is great because the last thing you want to do is show someone you have something for sale before they've been properly prepared to *want it*.

You leave a link to your sales page in that fifth email. Those that click that link immediately get bumped to yet another email list—the list of people that have viewed your sales page.

To simplify this, let's say there are three email subscribers, Tom, Dick, and Harry.

Tom doesn't open that fifth email. So he stays on the list and gets more emails encouraging him to check out the sales page until he finally clicks on it.

Dick and Harry are lovers, but they're in a terrible quarrel right now. Harry's really mad at Dick for being such an asshole. And Dick's really mad at Harry because he refused to get properly waxed, and Dick HATES stubble on his trouble.

Oh wait, that's something totally different. I'm talking about a different Dick and Harry. They're just some email subscribers. Sorry about the confusion there.

Dick clicks (No, I'm not talking about a Prince Albert, but yes, the Harry mentioned earlier totally has one of those, as do I of course—Mrs. Flogging wouldn't have it any other way) on the sales page link for your lower price-point offering. But he doesn't buy. So he is cast onto a different list where he receives a unique message like this:

> "Hi Dick,
>
> I know it can be hard to take the leap into buying something online. There are a lot of scams out there. I've fallen prey to about 100 of them! I gess I'm not the sharpess tool in the toolshid. That's whut mama always you sta say.
>
> Not funny? Yeah, my comedy skills peaked in about the 4th grade. It's pretty sad.
>
> Listen, I'm not a scammer, and the value I put into my *365 Days to Financial Freedom Workbook* is no joke. It's a powerful thing. You'll be saving more money *per day* by the end of the first month on what it will cost to buy it now. So I know it can't possibly be the fear of not getting your money's worth. You absolutely will.
>
> Is it the time and commitment required to fill out a workbook? Sounds like a homework assignment I

know. Yuck. I've turn to run from many a "workbook" over the years for that very reason.

Hey listen, no one understands the fear of taking on a new task better than I do. I've always got more on my plate than I can manage as is. And I doubt anyone has failed to implement something on a daily basis more than I have.

But this will be different I promise. You'll actually spend less time on money matters, and the anxiety and stress that you'll be able to relieve yourself of by being knowledgeable and informed about your financial health 7-days per week is something you have to experience to believe.

So please. Just try it. I believe in this so much, that's why I developed it and completely dedicated my life to getting it out to people—to save them from the crazy mistake I made by being so oblivious to my own finances.

If you have any questions or hesitations at all, please just reply to this email. I or someone on my team will respond in less than 24 hours (well, we try!).

If you're ready to change your life and be the master of your own financial destiny, pick up the workbook HERE."

If Dick still doesn't buy after that second email, he'll remain on that same list until he does, receiving a message daily until he either unsubscribes or finally gives it a shot.

Harry is different. He buys right away, and when he does buy the product, he gets bumped to a list of people who have purchased it. Now you can communicate with just your customers and deliver even more value and shock and awe coolness until they are primed to purchase, say, a $99 introductory coaching session with you to get a financial health evaluation.

But you of course wouldn't want to offer this to someone that hadn't even started using your workbook yet.

And, once someone had purchased an initial financial health evaluation, they could be bumped to yet another list where you could offer a premium course or full, 1-year coaching series on smart investing for thousands of dollars.

Sorry I keep referring to you like you're an online financial advisor. Hopefully speaking in specifics helps you envision it. It helps me explain it.

Does this help you see the power of segmentation and email sequences? It gives you so much more control, and it also gives you tremendous ability to convert your most stubborn subscribers into buying your introductory level product, which is huge. Selling stuff to a customer that's never purchased from you is much harder than selling more stuff to a customer you've already seduced with your relentless charm, humor, and good looks.

Customers are like sex really. It's a lot easier to talk someone into sex for the second, third, and fourth time than it is the first. It is for me at least, but you have to keep in mind that I'm highly skilled at it and have the proper gear to get the job done right.

And continuing with that theme (Would you expect anything less from me?), you can't expect someone you just met to have sex with you. Clearly there is a very small percentage of people who might, but to maximize your chances you need a lengthy courtship period to build trust and rapport.

And that's the beauty of sequences. They allow you to do that more elegantly. They allow you to do it more intimately, delivering the appropriate message to everyone at the perfect time. You're not trying to sell a product to subscribers that have already bought it. You're not pitching $1,000 consultations to someone that subscribed two days ago along with those that are already halfway through their consultation series with you.

With segmentation and sequences, because your messages are such a perfect fit for the subscriber— delivered with just the right timing—you'll see not only much better performance out of your email marketing, you'll have a lot less carnage as well. By carnage I mean people no longer opening or reading your emails or worse—unsubscribing altogether.

Really think about the power of segmentation and sequencing for your own personal business. I think with a little brainstorming, now that you understand the basic functionality, you'll start to realize the power of it.

So, how do you set up advanced sequencing and segmentation like that?

There are several webmail providers that offer this, but I think it only makes sense to set this up when you have multiple products and services at multiple price points. And if you have that, you'll likely want to have an affiliate program. Maybe you'll want some kind of membership and subscription set up, too. And you want to avoid bootstrapping several plugins and pieces of software to do that when you can get it all in one.

And that's why I recommend taking the leap to Ontraport. While I have word from Aweber (The gold standard in email broadcasting who I've used for years) that they'll be adding better sequencing and segmentation in the future, they are way behind the curve at the moment, and I don't expect they'll also integrate payment/checkout, memberships and subscriptions, affiliate tracking, and all the things that Ontraport does.

If you're familiar with internet business, you've probably heard about Infusionsoft. Ontraport is a lot like Infusionsoft. Some have even rated it more highly than Infusionsoft. Ontraport is like Infusionsoft's little brother. While the company is not as big, and Ontraport isn't as widely known, it's a much better fit for someone starting out.

With Infusionsoft, you're looking at a lengthy, mandatory training and set up that costs $2,000! Yikes! I've started entire businesses for far less than that. And after that you pay a hefty monthly fee to host and send emails. With Ontraport you have free training and a nice free trial period, and then you jump in at $297 per month (subject to change of course), which won't last long as you'll quickly grow enough to need their $597 plan for up to 100,000 email subscribers.

That's pretty tough to swallow as a beginner just getting going. It's hard to recommend it knowing you could get by with something a lot more primitive to start. But I know you'll get several more dollars out of each subscriber with Ontraport vs. a much cheaper service. A few extra dollars out of 1,000 subscribers will more than make up for the costs. Plus, setup is way easier, as you get your payment/checkout and affiliate stuff all included in one and a team on your side helping guide you to getting it all installed properly.

And even basic email delivery services with hardly any bells and whistles at all, like Aweber (2015), isn't cheap. Last month's bill inflamed my anus:

	Thank you for your payment!	
CHARGES		
Date	Description	Amount
April 10, 2015 to May 10, 2015	(Using 104240) Stores 26,000 Leads for $181.00, each additional 1,000 is $8.00	$ 813.00
	Total:	$ 813.00

My anus aside, please take advantage of the information I've just given you. I did the dumbest shit with my email service provider trying to save money. First, I started out with a company called Autoresponse Plus. I paid a few hundred bucks up front. After that, you were able to send unlimited broadcasts to unlimited subscriber numbers without ever paying a dime. That's where they managed to hook my scrotum and pull me into their shit parade.

I gathered subscribers and thought I was doing pretty well for myself. But I noticed something weird. I'd send out an email broadcast to 20,000 subscribers with a link to one of my latest blog posts, and my traffic would only rise by about 200 visits after doing that. Seemed a little odd.

Only when I finally made the jump to Aweber did I realize how shitty my Autoresponse Plus was. Aweber immediately informed me that my list was bogus—full of phony email addresses. No wonder all my messages were going to peoples' spam boxes, and no wonder my email broadcasts didn't affect my blog traffic like I thought it would. Only a few hundred people were both:

a) Real people
b) Actually having my emails make it through their spam filters

And so, when I switched over to Aweber after several years of building this supposed list, I had to start over again at ZERO. Years down the drain.

And while Aweber has been awesome, and it's really the only feasible option economically for Buck Books at the moment (I send millions of emails monthly, and they let you send as many as you like at no extra charge—they just charge you to store the email addresses), I too have outgrown its functionality.

Please don't go that route! Get something that fits loose that you can grow into, not something tight that you're going to grow out of. As an internet entrepreneur, you'll mature much faster with a better piece of equipment in your toolbox. Actually, Ontraport is the whole toolbox.

If I've learned anything, it's to pinch pennies like a mofo on basic life expenditures—housing, car, food, entertainment, shopping, etc.—but to spend freely to get premium shit and premium information when it comes to anything pertaining to your business. I'm not an extravagant guy (as evidenced by the 7-year old t-shirt I'm rocking at this moment with fist-sized holes in the armpits), and I've always made very economical decisions as an adult. But that characteristic really hurt me when it came to things like email service providers, hosting, web design, and a number of other things. It wasn't until I started spending big on my business that I started earning big, and that trend is accelerating the deeper I go down that path.

I'll spare you the rest of that tangent, but be cautious about spending money in the wrong places and not spending money in the right places. Both can bite you in the ass, a saying that reminds me of a really cool party I went to once back in college.

Fuck SPAM

I think that covers most of the information that I was really excited to share with you about email marketing. It's really fun. I love it. It's so easy and intuitive. But it's complex enough to also really geek out with it, which feels like a fun game at times. Armed with knowledge of your RPS (revenue per subscriber), and knowing how to use many of the primary bells and whistles of email marketing platforms like Ontraport, your success is destined to be greater and strike much faster.

But let me say a few things about SPAM. Calm down Hawaiians. I'm talking about "irrelevant or inappropriate messages sent on the Internet to a large number of recipients."

Don't take any chances with SPAM. You don't want your messages to begin showing up in a SPAM filter. If you do too much on the border of appropriateness and get a lot of complaints from your subscribers, you also run the risk of having your account completely shut down. Yes, it's scary, and yes, email service providers have the right to do that if some of their users are jeopardizing their email deliverability rates. So be smart, use common sense, and be careful.

The most important thing when it comes to SPAM is that the people you are sending to know and have volunteered to receive email messages from you. You will want to have them confirm their subscription after they've signed up, referred to as "double optin." Wherever they are subscribing, you'll want to mention openly that they will receive messages from you. You know, that whole honest and authentic thing coming back at you again.

To scare the shit out of you, here is the verbiage from Aweber's website on their anti-spam policy:

"This should go without saying, but we'll say it anyway: it's not OK to spam people. If you try, we will immediately close your AWeber account. You will not get any refund.

Chances are, you already knew spam is bad. And as an email recipient, you know it when you see it.

It's important that as a sender, you know what spam is, too. We'd hate to see you make the mistake of spamming anyone with your email marketing campaign.

So let's talk about what spam is and what happens if you do it at AWeber.

What Is Spam?

Ask 10 different people that question, and you'll probably get 10 different answers.

Email senders (like AWeber) tend to use the textbook definition: Unsolicited Bulk Email (UBE).

UBE is a useful definition: it points out that some things that might be OK to do on a 1-to-1 basis (like send an email about your company to someone who has never heard of you) are not OK to do in bulk.

But it's not a perfect one. Many things are not UBE but are considered spam by most people, including us.

Instead of trying to create a definition of spam that covers every possible scenario, let's look at a few things that we will consider spamming. We think this will give you a pretty good idea of what not to do.

Things You May Not Do With AWeber:

- Send email to people who have not specifically requested that information from you.
- If you collect subscribers somewhere other than on your website, and aren't 100% sure someone asked to sign up to your email lists, here's a helpful guide: http://bit.ly/1IsuAtU.
- Post irrelevant links to your website in discussion forums, newsgroups or classifieds sites like Craigslist.
- Use email lists that you purchased, rented, leased, or in any way bought from a third party. This includes email addresses that you purchased via co-registration.
- Send unsolicited email through a third party in order to try to get people to sign up to your AWeber-managed email list, or to visit a website that you market using AWeber in any way.
- This includes trying to get people to sign up on an AWeber web form that you have placed

on your website OR trying to get them to
email your AWeber email address.

- Batch or in any way try to script the addition
  of new subscribers to the web form subscribe
  methods. (You can learn more about this in
  our service agreement.)

These aren't the only things we might consider
spam. But they're a good guide.

Not sure if we'd consider something to be spam?
Contact us and find out!

What Happens If I Spam, Or Try To Spam?

If we find that you are spamming, or trying to spam,
with your AWeber account:

Things That Will Definitely Happen:

1. We will immediately terminate your account.
2. We will refuse to refund your account.

Things That Might Happen:

1. We might charge you money if your spamming
   causes any interruptions in our ability to service
   other customers.
2. We might pursue legal action against you.
   (Spamming violates our service agreement.)

Note: we don't presume guilt. We investigate all
potential spam incidents thoroughly before making a
decision. But once we've made a decision, we act fast."

Okay, so that was horrifying. Just don't get too clever or devious in capturing email addresses. Also don't get stupid with lots of ALL CAPS IN YOUR EMAIL BROADCAST OR EMAIL HEADLINE WITH ASSLOADS OF THESE THINGS ***** AND THESE >>>>>>>>AND DON'T EVEN GET TOO CARRIED AWAY WITH THESE!!!!!!!!!!!!

That's all folks. With a good lead capture page and some appropriate emails that you get permission to send and that are relevant to what subscribers were told they were getting when they signed up, you should be all good.

Email FAQ

How often should you send emails?

I usually send an email out every five minutes, so it feels like they're having a live chat with you. Kidding. Most people say once or twice per week is a good maximum for most things, unless you've explicitly stated that they are subscribing to get daily deals, discounts, news updates, or something that needs to come out that frequently.

I keep losing subscribers every time I send an email out. Is that bad?

It's unavoidable. Not everyone is going to love to hear from you. In reality, they're probably just busy, and they've got too many other emails competing for their attention with yours. It happens. When you send out an email, you're reminding the ones that have lost interest to unsubscribe. I wouldn't worry about it too much. You'll likely lose anywhere from 0.2% to 0.4% of your subscribers when you send out an email. So if you have 50,000 email subscribers let's say, that would be 100-200 subscribers unsubscribing whenever you send something out to all of them.

What's a good open rate and clickthrough rate?

I'd say that great open rates are higher than 30%, and good clickthrough rates are above 10%--meaning that if you leave one or several links in a broadcast, about a third of the people opening the email will actually engage with the email enough to click on one of the links that you drop. If you do even better than that, great! But you shouldn't be too worried if you're not quite at those levels.

But really this brings up a more important issue that I haven't discussed, which is subscriber freshness. The longer a person has been subscribed, the less likely they are to be engaged. That's just reality. I'm sure you've gotten really excited about something for a few months and then eventually lost interest. Actually, you may have done that with everything. It's normal. So if you're thinking that if you get 10,000 subscribers out of hosting an event on your site and that you'll be set for life, think again. Lists go through a decay process, and you'll get less and less out of those subscribers as time passes by. You always need new blood coming into the pipeline.

Subscriber lists are like schlongs really. It's not the size that counts, it's how young and fresh it is. That determines how much mileage you can get out of it before it wilts. Oh did I say schlongs? I meant flowers.

And I can't imagine a more appropriate ending to this book, so I'll have to skip the whole conclusion thing. It's perfect, as I hate saying what I've already said all over again. Stupid conclusions.

The Quit Your Job in 6 Months
Internet Business Course

Enjoy your Flogging experience? You must have if you made it this far. For a much more in-depth and up-to-date education on launching an internet business with quick and reliable success, take the Quit Your Job in 6 Months Internet Business Course.

Find out more at: www.QuitN6.com

Made in the USA
Columbia, SC
14 October 2018